TO:

FROM:

DATE:

What I Want You To Know
Messages Of Hope & Joy From Your Baby
Published by R.A. Hudson/Jar Of Moths
Copyright © 2013 R.A. Hudson. All Rights Reserved. No
part of this publication may be reproduced or transmitted
in any form or by electronic or mechanical means,
including photocopy, recording, information storage
and retrieval system, or digital media without written
permission from the Publisher except in the case of brief
quotations embodied in critical articles and reviews.
www.jarofmoths.com • www.rahudson.com
jarofmoths@gmail.com • 612.703.4944

First Edition

Printed in the United States of America

ISBN-13: 978-0615757872 (Jar Of Moths)
ISBN-10: 0615757871

WHAT I WANT YOU TO KNOW

MESSAGES OF HOPE & JOY FROM YOUR BABY

JAR OF MOTHS BOOKS

Grand Forks, North Dakota, U.S.A.

www.jarofmoths.com

About the Author & Illustrator

 R.A. Hudson has wanted to write and illustrate books ever since she was a child. Her illustrations and design work have appeared in many regional and national publications, as well as on the Internet.

R.A. lives in North Dakota with her husband, Rob, and youngest daughter, Presley, who has Down syndrome and is the original brave little messenger.

She can be contacted at **jarofmoths@gmail.com**

www.rahudson.com

Also By This Author:

 Get Creative! A Journal Journey
(Available at **www.rahudson.com**
as well as **www.amazon.com**)

*This one is for Presley,
who has shown me all of these messages
and will undoubtedly reveal many more.*

*Special thanks to my loving
& amazingly supportive husband, Rob.*

Having a new baby is an exciting time, full of unlimited possibilities. But what happens to those parents or expectant parents who are faced with raising a child with special needs - specifically Down syndrome? You might feel as though suddenly the future is full of limitations and enormous challenges you do not feel equipped to handle.

I know because I've been there. The moment I learned our youngest daughter was born with Down syndrome, I felt the world closing in around me. As the doctor spoke, I could hear nothing but my heart beating and feel a whirlwind of emotions: panic for her immediate health issues, fear over what this diagnosis meant for her future, and grief over losing the vision I had of what she was going to be.

Years have now passed, and when I look back, I wish I had known what a remarkable person our daughter would become. I want all new and expectant parents of children with Down syndrome to know that it is going to be alright. Your child wants you to know this too. I wrote this book to convey some of the most basic lessons my daughter has taught me, in the hopes that it calms the fears and offers parents a moment of heart-warming perspective. Your baby will love you, and you are going to love that kiddo more than you ever thought possible. *That* is everything I want you to know, and it's all that truly matters.

—R.A. Hudson

 ommy and Daddy, I want you to know that you don't have to be afraid. I am a little fighter.

You've maybe heard that raising me
will be difficult. You might be worried
that I will be sickly, or sad,
but actually I will be stronger
than you can even imagine and full of joy.

It's true: I will face some challenges,
but now, and for my whole life, I will face
obstacles with a stubborn optimism.

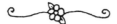

You were chosen to be my Mommy and Daddy.
You have strength and character within
you that you never knew existed. Because
of this, I know I can count on you to be my
advocate throughout my life. Sometimes
you will have to stand with me and blaze
paths fearlessly. I might need you to speak
up for me when my voice cannot be heard.

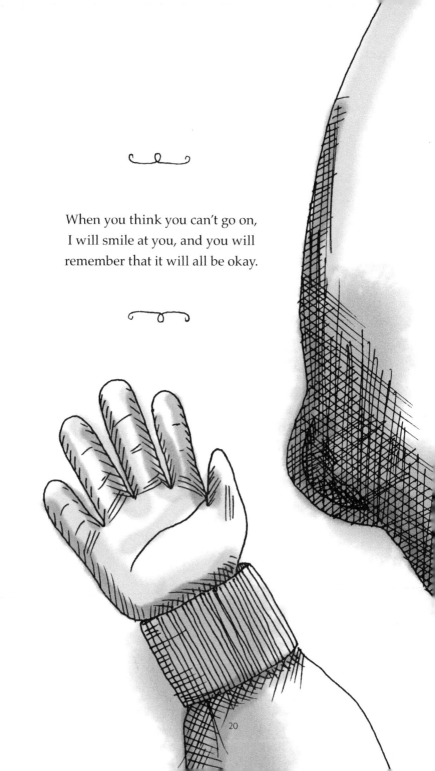

When you think you can't go on,
I will smile at you, and you will
remember that it will all be okay.

You may be wondering how much I
will be able to learn...but actually, I am
a teacher and you are a student.

I will be your shadow, and you will be
my hero. I won't even realize that you
feel the exact same way about me.

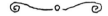

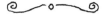

As I grow, you'll have new worries—far
more than I will. While you are worrying
if I will have friends, I will see the best
in everyone I meet. I will think every
stranger is just a friend I haven't yet met.

I will bring out kindness in others, and warm hearts. People will stop us in stores and tell you how they have a favorite niece or cousin with Down Syndrome. Or a child of their own. People you don't know will smile when they meet me for the first time.

I will be an individual. Ignore the stereotypes.

Some people will tell you how brave and strong you are...and they will be right.

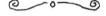

I won't be perfect. I will get into trouble and make you mad sometimes. I will probably break some things you once thought of as important. I will be sick when you had other plans. I will cry and get mad when you really need me to be good. I won't be perfect... but this is what all kids do sometimes.

You will peek in on me after you've tucked
me in for the night, and discover I'm sleeping
halfway out of the bed upside down.

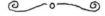

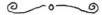

I will probably love music. As I grow, I
will want to dance with you, even at times
when you don't feel like dancing.
Or when you're too embarrassed to dance.
I won't be, and you shouldn't be either.

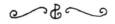

Other children and babies fascinate me.
I will be sure to point out every baby
and I will want to run and play with
any other child I see. I will probably let
you know whenever you drive past a
playground. I will want to stop and play.

I will always take time to stop and smell
the roses. And lilacs. And lilies. And
dandelions. And shrubs. And grass. And
trees. We don't have to hurry all the time.

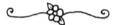

If you let me pick out my own clothes, you will
be amazed how great polka dots, stripes, and
a warm knit hat look together. In the summer.

You may be concerned about how I'll look,
and how people will have preconceived
ideas about me based on my appearance.
It is true. I will have certain characteristics
in my appearance that will make me stand out.
But I will also look like you.

You will be protective of me, and I need that. I won't always recognize or understand danger. You will say, "This kid is going to give me a heart attack!" But I'm really not *trying* to do that.

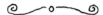

I will need you to help me control my
impulses. You can best teach me this by
example. If something tastes good, I will
want more. If something is fun, I will want
to do it over and over. I will probably pick a
video or song you find completely annoying
and make it my favorite. I will want to play
it again and again, and I won't understand
how you can't just make it magically come
out of every television or speaker.

I like to make a game out of everything. Everything. Time to get up and get dressed? Game. Meal time? Game. Running errands? Game. Walking from the car to the house? Game. Cleaning the house? Game. School? Game. Bedtime? Game.

Game.

Game.

Game.

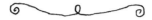

You can either play along or you can get
extremely frustrated. You know what I'd
suggest? A game. I seem to know one thing
very well: *You can never laugh and play enough.*

At some point, we might be faced with me
needing surgery: a valve fixed in my tiny
egg-sized heart…tubes in my ears…maybe
my eyes need to be corrected. I will have to
leave the worrying to you, as I will be far too
busy smiling and charming the doctors and
nurses. If I should happen to look concerned,
it's probably because I'm empathetic to
your tears or the fear I see in your eyes.

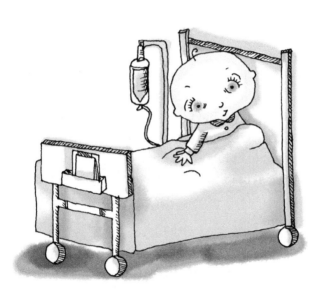

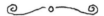

Let's be real, I probably won't make it to Harvard Medical School. Chances are, you didn't either. But I will go to school, and I will learn, and with your help, I can do anything I want to in life. Things may take me longer to master, but I will never give up unless you do.

As I grow, you may find that I probably
don't like change. I may have a difficult time
transitioning from one activity to the next. It
may be because I really like what we are doing
and don't want to stop. It may be because I don't
fully understand what you expect me to do
next. Let me know in advance, prepare me, and
if you can, make it fun. I do enjoy having some
control over my life too, so please understand
when our plans don't always work together.

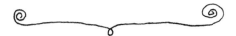

Any difficulties or challenges we face will be no match for us. The world is full of two types of people: those who love me, and those who don't know me. You now fall under the type "those who love me." I am lucky to have you for my Mommy and Daddy.

We are lucky to have one another.

One more thing....

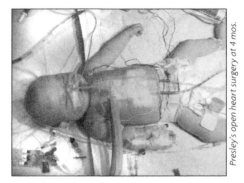

Presley's open heart surgery at 4 mos.

Soon you will look back at any long days spent like this as a hazy and distant memory...

...and when you get through those days, they will make all the rest even more cherished and precious.

THANK YOU

Once just a dream, now it's a book!
Big thanks to the amazing generosity of:

KIMBERLY BERGSTROM
BILL & JULIE HUDSON
PATRICK HUDSON
MIKE & PEG LUCAS
DEREK SAGGERS

& many others